GETTING AROUND IN WASHINGTON, D.C. BY SOUND

Published for the Benefit of
Tourist to Make Their Visit
Enjoyable — Plus Stories of Family
History and Personal Experiences
in the Capital City

By John Richard IHRIE III — 4th GENERATION

To order additional copies of this book, contact:
Xlibris
844-714-8691
www.Xlibris.com
Orders@Xlibris.com

ISBN: Softcover   978-1-4500-2676-5

Print information available on the last page

Rev. date: 05/07/2021

The designer of the federal capital city was Mayor Pierre Charles L´Enfant a French men, Friend and Confident of General George Washington

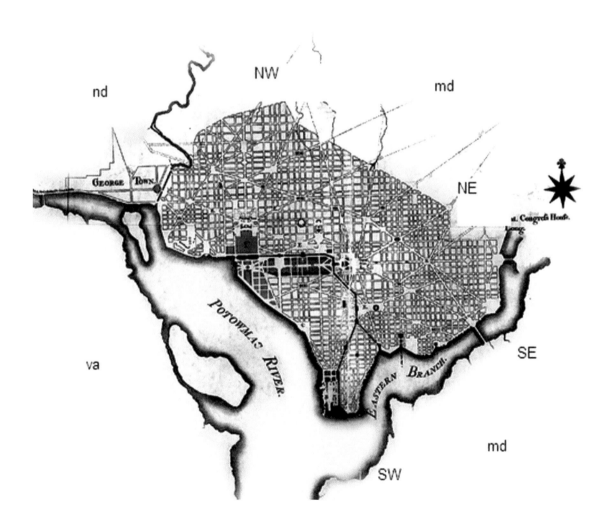

PREFACE

GETTING AROUND IN WASHINGTON, D.C. BY SOUND
THE KEY TO THE CITY

WELCOME TO WASHINGTON D.C., THE CAPITAL FEDERAL CITY
OF THE UNITED STATES OF AMERICA

I felt as a fourth generation, Washingtonian with Irish, Scottish, English and German ancestors that came to this Shores in the eighteen hundreds, I had to publish this paper back "THE KEY TO GETTING AROUND IN WASHINGTON D.C. OUR CAPITAL CITY BY SOUND!".

I hope you will enjoy my pocket book and L'Enfants code for getting around the Capital City with ease by using "THE KEY BY SOUND TO GETTING AROUND IN WASHINGTON D.C.", during your visit.

John R. Ihrie III
Artist – Author

CHAPTER ONE

It took fourteen years after the signing of the Decoration of Independence to put in place a plan by the founding fathers to select a permanent Capital for the new nation. Beginning to plan a Federal Capital City of which Mexico City is the other Federal Capital City.

George Washington and the founding fathers selected a site on the Potomac River (Pronounced "Pot o mac") and Indian name meaning "River of Swans", not far from Mount Vernon, George Washington's home. The man hired to plan a new capital city was a Frenchmen, Pierre Charles L´Enfant (who liked to be called "Peter"). He set about in the seventeen nineties to begin his work with the help of a surveyor, James Banneker. A former slave, freed and train by Lord Fairfax, an English man and George Washington, to become a surveyor. In the 1790's, He began his job traveling around the area as a surveyor for the new Capital City. Unfortunately sleeping in tents and working under hazardous conditions caused fevers delaying his work!

Washington and others began holding building lot sales events in "George's Town", named for the King George III, of England! However, they found that selling buildings lots in the new Federal City was not progressing as fast as they wish! George´s town later became know as George Town, part of the New Capital. Founded originally as a trading post in the sixteen hundreds with the Indians at what is now Wisconsin Ave & "K" ST.NW!

In order not to be able to develop the Virginia Land donated fast enough the founding fathers decided to give back to Virginia their land. The land that the Capital City stands on today was given by Maryland. The government of the District of Colombia in the Capital City today would like to have that land back which would will include Arlington and parts of Fairfax for a tax base! THAT WILL NEVER HAPPENDED!

The land running, along the Potomac River on the Virginia side is governed by the Department of Interior. Arlington Cemetery comes under the supervision of National Parks Administration.

CHAPTER TWO

TALKING ABOUT GETTING AROUND IN THE "FEDERAL CAPITAL CITY" BY "SOUND" WHICH HAPPENS TO BE A "PET" "EXPRESSION OF THE AUTHOR"!

Pierre L'Enfant did a spectacular job in planning the city. He put the Capital Building facing East in the center as a "Hub". Four quadrants, NORTHWEST, NORTHEAST, SOUTHWEST and SOUTHEAST. Each quadrant has streets running North, South, East and West! The North and South streets are new numerical, the East and West are alphabetical. The quadrants are divided by North Capital, South Capital and on East Capital and Avenues in the south such as Independence and Constitution.

Each quadrant in the alphabetical section begin with one syllable such as "A", two syllable such as Aspen or three syllabuses Albemarle Street in the northwest quadrant . If I said to you go to thirty Ninth and Livingston Street! Northwest, By sound, you would know you are in the third alphabet of the Northwest quadrant at thirty nine street. Livingston ST, If you where looking for a friend at thirty nine twenty four Livingston, you would look to the right and the property would be on the South side which carries even numbers. On the North side of the street are the odd numbers such as thirty nine twenty five. This situation exits in every quadrant. All you have to know is the quadrant that you want to be in e.g. NORTHWEST, NORTHEAST, SOUTHWEST and SOUTHEAST and then the street which it is one, two or three syllable words. You will know by sound according to what hundred block you wish to be in. Whether it be the one hundred block or the fifteen hundred block, etc.!

The third alphabet in any quadrant begin with three syllable words e.g., Albemarle Street Northwest. This begins the third alphabet in the Northwest quadrant. When the third alphabet reaches the end of the three syllable word e.g., Whittier Street Northwest it begins again with two syllabus names e.g., Aspin Street Northwest on Sixteen Street in the Northwest quadrant until the two syllable words continue alphabetical until it reaches the Maryland State line!

The Avenues were designed off the Capitol building "Hub" like the spokes of a wheel. Being French, L'Enfant sort to bring the great Avenues of Paris, his home country to be implemented into the new Federal Capital City of the United States of America. Names for the Avenues were chosen from the States e.g. Pennsylvania, Massachusetts, Virginia, Maryland etc.! Names for avenues were chosen from States and Historical documents e.g. Independence and Constitution.

If I say to you "go to the one hundred block of A Street Northeast", by "SOUND" you will know how to get there following L'Enfant's code. You will know it is in the Northeast quadrant off East Capital Street the dividing line between Northeast, Southeast, one block from the Capital building after New Jersey Avenue. You would turn North on first street Northeast, "A Street" would be the first Street on your right and you will find that you were in the one hundred block of "A Street" Northeast. Even numbers on the South side of "A street", uneven numbers on the North side of "A street".

Using L'Enfant's code you can find your way in the city by "SOUND". Remembering four quadrants each quadrant three sections one, two and three syllable words. In the section that is the quadrant you are looking for! Remembering Numerical Streets run North and South. Alphabetical streets run East and West. THIS WAY KNOWING, THESE THINGS MAKE IT IMPOSSIBLE TO GET LOST.

In the same way getting around by SOUND for Avenues it's a little tricky. Being at the Capital and First Street Northwest Massachusetts Avenue. If I say I will meet you at the COSMOS CLUB for lunch at Twenty Third Street and Massachusetts Avenue Northwest. You will know by SOUND that you have to follow Massachusetts Avenue Northwest until you get to Twenty Third Street, Numerical streets (running North and South). Now comes the tricky part normally when you come to Circles, on your way normally you make a half circle and you still be on Massachusetts Avenue, however seventh street and ninth street are a little difficult to go around and continue on Mass Avenue! After you get around that area continuing on Massachusetts Avenue you take the underpass between thirteen and fourteen Streets. Following on to sixteen street and General Scott circle, where you will make again Half Circle and continue on Mass, Avenue until you get to Dupond Circle. Again Half circle pick up Massachusetts Avenue continue on to Twenty - Third street. The Cosmos Club will be on your right. It's a Professional Membership Club.

L'Enfant's code made an important contribution to our Capital City. "BY SOUND YOU CAN ALWAYS KNOW EXACTLY WHERE YOU ARE OR WHERE YOU ARE GOING."

CHAPTER THREE

THE AUTHORS STORIES OF GROWING UP IN THE FEDERAL CITY AND HIS EXPERIENCES AS A FOURTH GENERATION WASHINGTONIAN.

My great-grandfather William Collins came from county Mayo, Ireland in the eighteen forties and settle in the Capital. Building, his home and business as a blacksmith, at 218F street North West. My mother saved her father's families funeral bills from the eighteen hundreds reflecting anywhere from $500 to $1000 dollars deaths, occasion by epidemics in the city!

On the maternal grandmother side they where Branson from England. Her brother, Taylor Brandson, was brought into the Marine Band by John Phillip Sousa. Later he became Marine Band Leader!. On my father's mothers side the Oliphant's of Scotland came in the eighteen hundred. My great grandfather, James Oliphant fought in the cavalry during the Civil War in the Eighteen Sixties. He is buried in Arlington cemetery in direct line with the "Mass of the Maine".

In the thirty's, at twelve years of age I remember taking the street car on Saturday mourning for a Nichol and going to visit my paternal grandmother "Rosa Oliphant Ihrie" at 1302 Monroe Street Northwest (second alphabet). We would have lunch and a game of Parcheesi or Monopoly. Later she would give me a quarter and her sister, Mary Oliphant another quarter. I would go to the TIVOLI theater matinee for $0.25 cents. I would fall off my seat laughing at "Laurel and Hardy" and "Thelma Todd", "Patsy Kelly" "Comedy Movies"!

After the movie, on Saturday in the 30's I would cross Park Road at fourteen street Northwest to a carry-out. Mr. J. Willard Marriott would be cooking hamburgers on the grill. He would hand me, out the window a hamburger and root beer for $0.10 cents. I would go back to my grand mother house before returning home on the street car for $0.05

Every inaugural my mother would take me to the U.S. capital building to watch the President of the United States being Sworn-in and other festivities that followed with a Parade down Constitution Avenue to Pennsylvania Avenue Northwest. We would be standing in a little Iron Shelter watching the events designed by the famous landscaper of the Capital Ground. The President would wave to the crowds and begin his ride to the White House. My first Presidential swearing in was, Franklin Delano Roosevelt in Nineteen Thirty Two .

I remember as a child in the twenty's seeing Mrs. Calvin Coolidge ride down Pennsylvania Avenue in her electric car unattended on her way to the Capital for lunch. The car was designed so that you couldn't tell the front from the back. The only way you could tell the front is by the way the car was headed. The next President I remember was Herber Hoover, who after World War One helped Europe recover through agricultural assistance. Roosevelt followed in Nineteen Thirty Two.

I remember when the banks closed in Washington D.C. during the depression, 1929. My maternal grandmother, Eva Branson Collins was very upset! She had to wait three days before the banks reopen for business. She could not draw funds!

The depression brought a group of veterans from World War One to Washington, called "Cox's Army". They build shacks along the Anacostia River and Petitioned Congress for benefits. When they didn't leave the city in a reasonable time the U.S. Cavalry was brought in to destroy the shacks and moved the veterans out. They returned to their homes.

Washington D.C. in the thirties was a sleepy small city. In the forties it was beginning to grow. After December 7th, 1941, when Japan attack Pearl Harbor, it became a Bustling City. I entered military servers in 1942 and served in the same Coast Guard service with my father who also fought in World War I on board the U.S.S. Cunningham, whose port was Cork, Ireland, protecting shipping lanes from German Submarines!

My parents are buried in Arlington National Cemetery near the family Plot of George's Washington Park Custis and his wife Mary, original owners of Arlington House also known as the Custis-Lee Mansion.

My great grand father, James Oliphant, fought in the Civil War and is buried in direct line with the "Mast of the Main", a ship which went down in the Spanish-American War in Havana, Cuba in the 1890's.

In the nineteen seventies I stood on my great grand father grave site and painted a pastel of the "Mast of the Main". In Nineteen Ninety One, it was accepted by the Polish Government and returned to Warsaw, Poland, on Air Force One with the remains of "Jan Ignace Paderewski", Polish Statement and International Pianist! His remains had been placed in the turret, holding pen for dignitaries by President, Franklin Delano Roosevelt. Germany had invaded Poland and he could not be returned until a later day. That day was June, Fifth Nineteen Ninety One, when by invitation I went to the Polish embassy in Washington D.C. and made my gift presentation!

CHAPTER FOUR

Returning to Washington in the middle sixty's after a fifteen year career in New York City I began to paint series art in pastel. Industrial and Historical sites, Georgetown, "K" Street, Water front, before Industrial Plants came down and the Washington Harbor went-up!.

I reordered old buildings of Washington in the Seventeen's and Eighty's, one in particular "PARK & BRADGITTE", Ninth street and Pennsylvania Avenue N.W. (North east corner), in Nineteen Eighty Four. Where my great aunt, Nan Collins, clerked with Julius Garfanckel in 1910.

Later she became a buyer when he opened his first store at Eleventh and "F" Streets N.W., opposite Woodward & Lothrop. He became known as "Merchant Prince of Washington". He always maintain a close relationship with his customers and employees. On many occasions with customers in his store he would used his little book to write down any request his customers had for purchasing items on his next buying trip abroad.

CHAPTER FIVE

My web site www.pastellerybyIhrie.com, has paintings of New York, "Metropolitan Opera" Opening Night Philharmonic Hall now known as the "Alice Tully Hall" Lincoln center. Met Opening Night "Inner & Outer Halls ", (plus sketch) are available to Celebrate the "Fiftieth Anniversary in 2012".

FIRST INTERNATIONAL ART SHOW
CATHOLIC UNIVERSITY QUITO – ECUADOR NOVEMBER 15th, 2007

In 2007 my government sponsored me in my First International Art Show in Quito, Ecuador co-sponsored by the Culture Department of Catholic University of Quito and opened on November fifteen 2007, by the US Ambassador Linda Jewel. A great night of appreciation on my part!

My Galapagos Island creature's series of eight works on exhibit valued by the artist at ten thousand dollars was donated to the Catholic University Cultural Department. For the benefit when sold to present emerging Indian and Spanish Artist works of Ecuador. Artist exhibiting in local Parks providing them with an introduction to the public. The US Cultural attache's office & Director of the Cultural Dept. of the Catholic University of Quito to select the three or four Artist each year to be chosen for Exhibition from Park Artist.

Washington D.C., CITY CLUB, FIRST ARTIST PRESENTATION FEBREARY 2009

The City Club of Washington chose me as the first Washingtonian Artist under their Art Program to present his Art & Collection, February to July 2009 program, Marketing friends Douglas and Mary-Jo Shackelford helped to present forty works of art my paintings and collection, including paintings of Ecuador. Part of my Jerusalem and Palestine series of the Nineteen Century, where on show. This series was painted to honor my wife's family "The Khadders" of Jerusalem Palestine.

CHAPTER SIX

TRAVELING TO ECUADOR FOR MY SECOND VISIT AUGUST 18th 2009

I regard Ecuador and my Amigos in particular, the Larrea Family and my friend Oswaldo Vallejo as my second home. My thrust is to help promote the art works of Artists in the Parks with the help of my governments Cultural Attache in Quito and the Cultural Department of Catholic University in Quito, Gaby Costa, Director who was very instrumental in promoting my art show of Colonial Quito and Galapagos Island Creatures in November 2007.

I hope to be able to begin the process of this project with the help of my friends and the cultural attaches office of the U.S. government here in Quito and at the Cultural Department of Catholic University in Quito before I return to the U.S.

My marketing friends the Shackelfords are scheduling an art show opening of twenty pastels and drawings of old buildings in Washington D.C., painted in the Seventy's, for an exhibit at the U.S. Chamber of Commerce "H" Street N.W. near the White House when I return to Washington in October 2009.

I hope you have enjoyed my commentaries on life in "The Big City". My idea of "THE KEY TO GETTING AROUND IN WASHINGTON, OUR CAPITAL FEDERAL CITY BY SOUND", has made your visit pleasant and interesting. It is one of the Great Capital Cities in its infancy, one of two Federal Cities in the World, the other Mexico City. I truly love my City and like to share it with visitors.

Respectfully,
John Richard Ihrie III
ARTIST – AUTHOR

OLD BUILDINGS OF WASHINGTHON, D.C.

BY ARTIST

JOHN RICHARD IHRIE III

COLOR PLATE NUMBER ONE

"HEURICH HOUSE"

HEAD QUARTERS FOR THE

HISTORICAL SOCIETY OF WASHINGTON, D.C.

(47 YEARS)

Built in the Eighty Nineties by Christian Heurich

German Breuer-Heurich Beer

Artisans from Germany Carved work in the Mansion

Heurich House
Historical Society of Washington D.C.- 1956-2003

COLOR PLATE NUMBER TWO

PARK & BRIDGETTE SPECIALLY STORE – 19TH CENTURY BUILDING LOCATED AT 9TH STREET & PENNSYLVANIA AVENUE, NORTHWEST NORTH EAST CORNER.

The building was demolish in Nineteen Eighty Four. The artists decided to painted it for family connections as described previously in this book.

COLOR PLATE NUMBER THREE

THE DE - MONET BUILDING – CONNECTICUT AVENUE, "M",

AT RHODE ISLAND AVENUE N.W.

INTERESTING ARCHITECTURE OF THE 19TH CENTURY

COLOR PLATE NUMER FOUR

"ARLINGTON HOUSE"

Also known as the "CUSTIS-LEE MANSION"

Today this property is known as Arlington National Cemetery with many monuments to "Honor the Defenders of our Liberty" which we are now privileged to enjoy!

ORIGINAL PEN & INK DRAWINGS

When the Artist paints a famous landscape he does not paint the famous overview of the subject, but instead paints his interpretation of the landscape from a different angle.

PEN & INK NUMBER ONE

GEORGE WASHINGTHONS HEAD QUARTERS, GEORGES TOWN 1776.

Georges Town was named in honor of King George III of England and later became know as George Town in the Capital City

PEN & INK NUMER TWO

FIRE BOAT – POTOMAC RIVER CHANNEL IN THE 1970.

S.W. WATER FRONT, WASHINGTHON, D.C.

PEN & INK NUMBER THREE

SMITH SONIAN TOWER

"PREPARING FOR POPE JOHN PAUL´S VISIT 1979"

PEN & INK NUMBER FOUR

VIEW OF WASHINGTON D.C. FROM POTOMAC RIVER BOAT "DANDY"

Turning at the Kennedy Center a Panoramic view of Washington and the Cathedral,

heading back to Alexandria Virginia.

The Artist had many pleasant evenings dining and dancing on the Dandy, his Real State

Broker invested in this service for visitors during the Bicentennial Year 1976.

CHAPTER SEVEN

THE MONUMENTS TO GEORGE WASHINGTON
(FOUR)

FIRST MONUMENT

The First Monument was erected and dedicated by the citizens of a small town Boonsboro, Maryland, on July 4th, 1824. It's shaped in the form of a milk bottle. Built out of stones from South Mountain. You can take the cheese cake steps like going up in a Castle and when you get to the top you will view three states Maryland, Virginia and West Virginia. During the Civil War this advantage point changed hands fourteen or more times between the Union and Confederate Forces battling in the Shenandoah Valley.

SECOND MONUMENT

The Second Moment is located in Baltimore Maryland at Mt. Vernon Square and Charles Street across from Peabody Institute. On the base of the monument are these words "THE FIRST MONUMENT OF ANY CONSEQUENCE BEGUN & COMPLETED TO THE MEMORY OF GEORGE WASHINGTON".

THIRD MONUMENT

The Third Monument is our National monument on the National Mall, Washington D.C. It was began in 1840 by the U.S. CORP of Engineers on land that was originally Swampland. Construction was stopped during the Civil War. Reconstruction began in the late 1860 when the CORP had to reinforce the foundation before they could, proceed building the Monument. The first person from the public was not able to go up in the Monument until 1885. Although the Monument itself was completed in 1880 with the Capping Ceremony. My grand father who was in construction had a friend who put the pinnacle point in place which I now have in my possession!

FOURTH MONUMENT

The Fourth Monument is in Alexandria Virginia, built by the Mason's called The Masonic Temple. George Washington was a prominent Mason. This monument is beautifully located and full of Mural Art Works.

FIRST MONUMET TO GEORGE WASHINGTON
Boonsboro Maryland
1824

SECOND MONUMET TO GEORGE WASHINGTON
Baltimore Maryland

THIRD MONUMET TO GEORGE WASHINGTON
National Monument on the National Mall

FOURTH MONUMET TO GEORGE WASHINGTON
Masonic Monument to George Washington Alexandria Virginia

SPECIAL NOTE OF APPRECIATION TO:

JUAN JOSE LANDAZURI SANCHEZ

QUITO, ECUADOR

FOR HIS HELP IN COMPUTER SET UP OF

FIRST DRAFT OF MY PAPER BACK BOOK

- J.R. IHRIE

Printed in the United States
by Baker & Taylor Publisher Services